THE
SHERINGHAM LIFEBOATS
1838~2000

by Mick Bensley

BENGUNN

2003

By the same author:
Watercolours of Norfolk Past
Watercolours of Sussex Past
The Rescues of Henry Blogg

*For Aimee, Russell
and all Lifeboatmen*

First published in 2003 by BENGUNN

Design and typography by Mick Bensley

Illustrations ©Copyright 2003 Mick Bensley

ISBN 0-9533998-1-8

All rights reserved. No part of this publication may be reproduced, stored in a retrieval system, or transmitted in any form or by any means, electronic, mechanical, photocopying, recording or otherwise, without the prior permission of the copyright holder. Pictures in this publication may not be displayed in any manner other than as bound in herewith.

Typeset in Palatino and
printed in England by Hartington Fine Arts Ltd., Lancing, Sussex

Contents

Foreword by Henry "Joyful" West, BEM · 5
Introduction by Robin and Linda West · 6
Artist's Preface · 10

RESCUES DEPICTED IN THE PAINTINGS

Dygden of Abo	12-13	*Uller* (Launch)	52-53
Nautilus of Aberdeen	14-15	*Uller* towing J.C. Madge	54-55
Villa Franca	16-17	*Ingeborg* of Helsingborg	56-57
Alert	18	*Boston Trader* of Gt. Yarmouth	60-61
Carolina	19	*Czajk* of Poland	62-63
Hero of Maldon	22-23	*Gold* of Rochester	64-65
Frances Ann of Goole	24	*Zor* of Istanbul	66-67
Trusty of Boston	25	*Wimbledon*	68-69
Wells of Goole	26	*Wimbledon*	70-71
Alpha of Faversham	27	*Windsor Rose*	72-73
6 Fishing boats	30-31	*Lucy*	76-77
Commodore	32-33	*Richmond Castle*	78-79
Ispolen	34-35	*Sallie*	80-81
Teutonic	36	*Harvester/Concorde II*	82-83
Teutonic and *Gothic*	37	*Force 4 GT*	84-85
Empress of Sunderland	38-39	*Tor Gothia*	86-87
Fishing boats	42-43	*Alison Cathleen*	90-91
Henry Ramey Upcher	44	*Dory*	92-93
Asteroid of London	45	Bibliography and Acknowledgements	95
Gothic	48-49	RNLI Awards to Sheringham Lifeboatmen	96
Lord Morton of London	50-51		

4

Foreword

Saving life from the sea at Sheringham was carried out by the private lifeboats in the early days. The *Augusta* lifeboat was provided by the Upcher family before the RNLI opened a station, and the first RNLI lifeboat arrived. The fishing village then had two lifeboats, both pulling and sailing, crewed by fishermen.

Launching against all that the North Sea could throw at them took tremendous effort and courage. Often a haul-off rope was needed to pull the lifeboat to sea, and at times it was necessary to double man the oars. The reward was that many crews were saved from vessels just before they foundered.

There were several RNLI pulling and sailing lifeboats, and these were always launched from a carriage, whilst the private lifeboats put to sea on skeets or rollers and boards, using the quant once the crew were aboard. The private and RNLI pulling and sailing lifeboats worked together for many years until 1936 when Sheringham had its first RNLI motor lifeboat and the town's last pulling and sailing lifeboat was retired.

The first motor lifeboat *Foresters' Centenary* became the wartime lifeboat and saved many airmen who ditched in the North Sea, as well as the crews of vessels damaged by enemy action. After the war, *The Manchester Unity of Oddfellows*, one of a new generation of self-righting lifeboats, served as a fine station boat for nearly 30 years, and Sheringham's last offshore lifeboat *Lloyds II* made its final launch in 1992.

Sheringham now has a fast Atlantic 75 Inshore lifeboat *Manchester Unity of Oddfellows* continuing the work, begun in 1838 by the *Augusta*, of saving life at sea.

In Mick Bensley's early years, he was often to be seen on the seafront at Sheringham, watching the fishermen launch their boats from the beach. He saw at first hand the boat builders at work, shaping the double-ended boats that were the only type that could be worked from the steep open beaches on this part of the Norfolk coast. As a painter, he has used that local knowledge to good effect, as the reader will find in this book. Every boat and lifeboat depicted has been minutely observed, and can be recognised and named by the families who used them.

I feel honoured to be asked to write the foreword for this book of Mick Bensley's paintings that are second to none.

Henry 'Joyful' West

Henry 'Joyful' West BEM

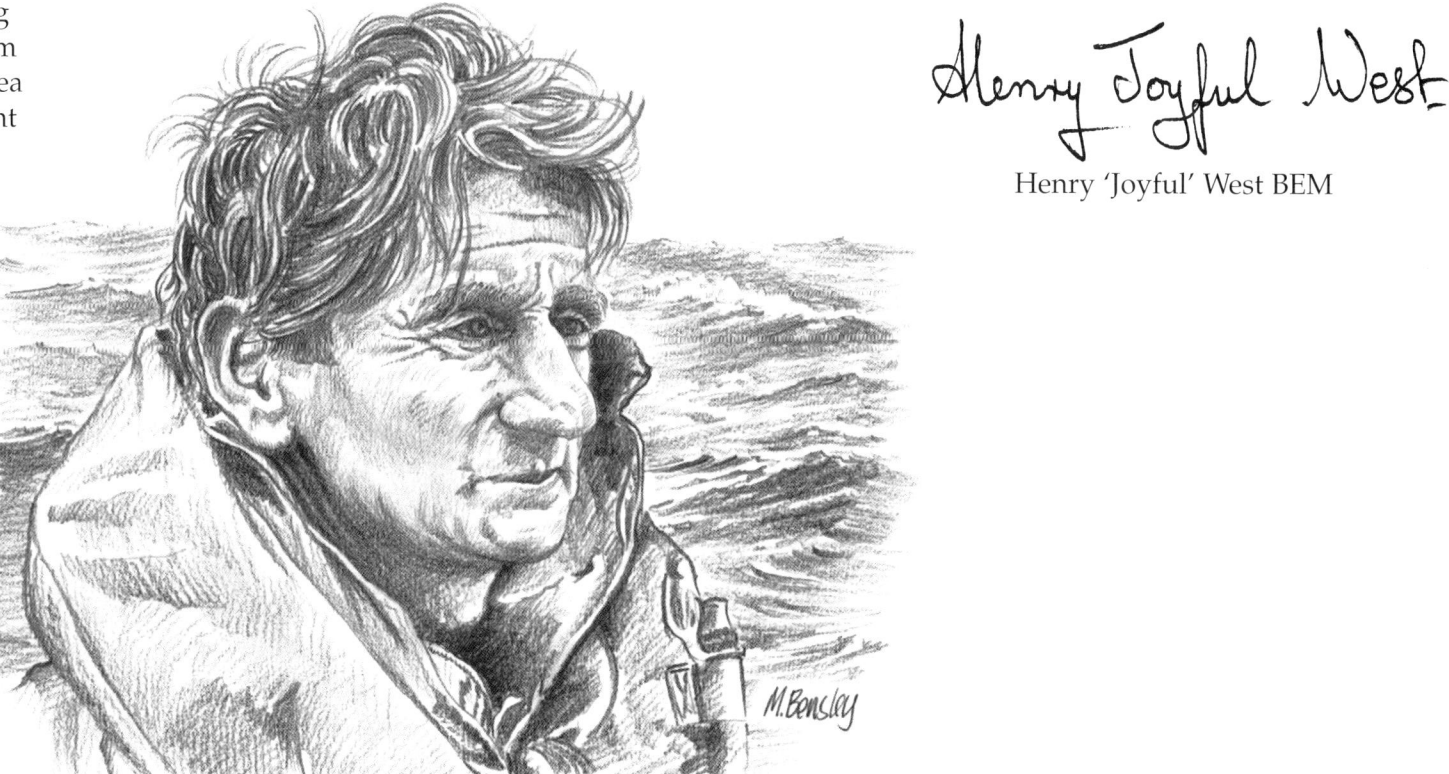

Introduction

by Robin and Linda West

The seaside town of Sheringham lies on the North Norfolk Coast some 25 miles north of Norwich. Its history as a settlement goes back many centuries; in the 1940s a number of gold coins were found scattered along the beach between Sheringham and Weybourne which were dated to around 65BC whilst Roman antiquities from the second century AD have also been found in the area. At the date of the Domesday survey the Manor of Silingham, as it was then named, was recorded to be one league long and one broad (ie seven miles in each direction) and from then its successive land-owners can be traced through the centuries until its purchase by the Upcher family, who became great benefactors of the town during the 19th century. Prior to the coming of the railways in 1887, inshore fishing and the trades dependent on it, such as sail-makers, rope-spinners and net-makers, provided the main employment for inhabitants of the town and visitors today will still see fishermen and their craft engaged in the crabbing industry.

Sheringham fishermen considered themselves a breed apart. Many of the fishing families can trace their ancestries back over two hundred years, and in the records the same surnames recur; Cooper, Craske, Grice, West, Bishop and Little, amongst others, have been found among the fishermen and lifeboat crews since the days of the private lifeboats. The same forenames can also be found many times over: Robert, George, Henry, and James were very common and were sometimes given to succeeding generations of a family who could all be involved in fishing at the same time. Under these circumstances it is no wonder that nicknames evolved over the years to distinguish individuals and their families. For example, in the crew at the naming of the *Henry Ramey Upcher*, there were 6 Coopers, 4 Bishops, 4 Wests, 3 Grices and 2 Craskes. Among the nicknames of the crew were 'Old Barnes' (Cooper), 'Loady' (West), 'Claxton' (West), 'Click' (Bishop) and 'Boots' (Johnson}. Their use has survived into recent times, with coxswains of, for example, the *Foresters' Centenary* including 'Sparrow' (Hardingham) and 'Downtide' (West).

In the early nineteenth century, the Upcher family of Sheringham Hall supplied loans to enable the local fishermen to build larger fishing boats to follow the herring shoals. One of these boats, the *Upcher*, built for Harry West, was launched in 1826 and a couple of years later was involved in the rescue of nine sailors from a wrecked vessel. Prior even to this, Abbot Upcher recorded in his journal for 1816; *"On the 1st September there was a perfect hurricane. On our own shore there were three ships wrecked whose crews, by the Gallantry of the Lower Sheringham men in Captain Manby's Life Boat were all saved."* These ships were the *Selby* of Sunderland, the *Hannah* of Shields and the *Oronoko* of Ipswich. All three ships were completely wrecked and a fourth was seen to founder off the town before any assistance could be given. Twelve ships are

THE 'UPCHER' GOING TO THE AID OF A SHIP IN DISTRESS. CIRCA 1828.

recorded to have been lost that night between Blakeney and Sheringham alone, all part of a fleet of 300 colliers and merchantmen seen passing along the coast the previous evening.

It was yet another severe storm and loss of life in 1836 which caused the Hon. Mrs. Charlotte Upcher to present the fishermen of Sheringham with a lifeboat built to the same design as the crab-boats, only on a larger scale. The *Augusta* was constructed by local builder Robert Sunman in a shed on the Sheringham Hall Estate. Like the crab-boats she was provided with 'orruck' holes in the top strake of the hull through which the oars were worked, and also with a mast for sailing. Uniquely for a lifeboat, the double-ended hull had fixings for the rudder at both ends which reduced the necessity for turning the boat in a heavy sea. She was launched on 14th November 1838 at Lower Sheringham, under Coxswain Robert Long who remained in charge for around twenty years. She had a proud tradition of service whilst on station, being credited with over 1000 lives saved. A proper written record of her launches was not kept at the time but research has established that she saved over 200 lives in 15 of her service launches.

The RNLI recognised the dangers of this stretch of coast when they sent the *Duncan* lifeboat, a 36' carriage launched self-righting type, to the town in 1867. The *Duncan* was housed at a boathouse behind the Mo, not far from the new Lifeboat Museum building. Unfortunately the access provided to the sea was narrow, and awkwardly positioned for launching, so not all the attempts to launch resulted in effective services. One of these attempts was to the *Alpha* of Faversham which was wrecked on 4th October 1883 off Cromer

Teddy 'Lux' Craske

and although the Cromer lifeboat launched, it was unable to reach the schooner due to the strength of the sea. Cromer rocket brigade was also called out, but the wind was too strong to allow it to make contact with the wreck by rocket. Messages were sent to Sheringham and the *Duncan* was taken overland to Runton to try to assist. Unfortunately when she reached Runton the tide was running too high for the boat and her carriage to be negotiated down the gangway. The *Alpha's* crew were finally saved when the vessel split in two and was pushed closer to the shore by the seas. Two Sheringham fishermen and a coastguardsman from Cromer waded into the surf with lines and the five man crew were brought ashore.

In 1885, local fishermen met with members of the RNLI Branch Committee and expressed their opinion that the *Duncan* was not ideal for Sheringham as she was too heavy. The RNLI was asked for a new, lighter boat and it was agreed that three of the fishermen should go to London to visit the Institution's boatyard to see if there were a suitable boat. They chose the *William Bennett*, another self-righting boat which, though narrower in beam, was both longer and heavier than the *Duncan*. Her masts sails and rig were designed in Sheringham, and the plans were sent to the Institution's yard for construction. The new boat arrived at Sheringham by sea on 7th July 1886, her carriage however had not arrived although it had been sent ahead – by rail. Then, when the new boat was being hauled up to the boathouse for the first time, the new winch gave way which did not impress the assembled dignitaries including the Chief Inspector and the RNLI Chairman Colonel Fitzroy Clayton. The *William Bennett* was stationed at Sheringham for eighteen years, but by then the slipway had become so dangerous due to storm damage that it was dismantled and the lifeboat was taken from the boathouse and kept ready for launch in Beach Road. After a couple of years wood rot had begun to set in, but this did not prevent her making a final and very arduous service to the steam yacht *Asteroid* on 10th September 1903. The *William Bennett* was launched into massive seas with a double crew and despite being almost overwhelmed half a mile from shore and losing two oars was able to reach the *Asteroid* and take her in tow for Great Yarmouth.

The *Augusta* lifeboat worked alongside the RNLI boats for over twenty years, but by the early 1890s her iron nails were beginning to deteriorate, so in 1894 Mrs. Caroline Upcher agreed to fund the cost of a replacement. The new boat was named *Henry Ramey Upcher* after Mrs. Upcher's late husband and was built by Lewis Emery in a shed at the West End, close to where she can be seen today. She was launched on 4th September 1894, and for the next thirty years she also worked closely with the RNLI boats to save life from both the fishing boats and merchant vessels in danger off the town. The *Henry Ramey Upcher's* most famous rescue was undoubtedly that of the crew of the *Ispolen*, but more typical are the rescues of the local fishermen and their boats which made her well known along that stretch of the Norfolk coast. The RNLI lifeboat crews' main priority has always been to save life, and while this may mean assisting in the salvage of a disabled vessel if that is the most efficient way to rescue the crew, in most cases the crew will be taken into the lifeboat, and their vessel left to be dealt with later when conditions allow. The *Henry Ramey Upcher* however, had been gifted by Mrs. Upcher into the ownership of the Sheringham fishermen and so operated differently. She would transfer not only the fishermen, but their nets, gear and catch, into the lifeboat. Then some of the lifeboat crew, equipped with lifejackets, would board the boats and the *Henry Ramey Upcher*, would tow them closer inshore to a point at which they could be safely beached. Most fishermen would volunteer for either Institution or private lifeboat and so there was stiff competition to get one of the lifebelts for both craft when called. A few fishermen such as 'Coaley' Cooper, the coxswain of the *Henry Ramey Upcher* from 1898 to about 1915, only ever sailed in one of the lifeboats.

In the summer of 1903 the local RNLI Committee asked the RNLI for a replacement for the *William Bennett*. Once again a delegation from amongst the crew was appointed, which consisted of the RNLI Coxswain, 'Click' Bishop, and two crew members R. H. Grice and C. Grice who visited other lifeboat stations along the coast to view the types of boat available. The delegation left the town with the intention of discovering a boat "of the non-self righting type and of a broader and lighter kind" (than the *William Bennett*). The final request to the RNLI however was for a boat "of the Liverpool type of larger dimensions if possible than the one at Cromer". The *J.C. Madge*, which arrived by sea from Blackwall on 2nd December 1904 fulfilled that request completely, being the longest pulling and sailing Liverpool type lifeboat built for the RNLI. A new corrugated iron lifeboat house was built at Old Hythe, a natural dip in the cliffs about a mile west of the town. At night, or in winter, this was a considerable distance for the crew to cover before the boat could be launched. Manpower was still essential in re-housing the 41-foot Liverpool class lifeboat, and the manually operated winch in the lifeboat house required many strong arms to turn the large handles as the boat was slowly recovered up the steep shingle banks. Unfortunately the sandy beach at Old Hythe proved to be too soft for the lifeboat and carriage and much work had to be carried out to level the shingle ridges which built frequently in front of the lifeboat house. Consequently when a new motor lifeboat was sent to Sheringham, a third site was chosen for the Institution boathouse at the west end of the promenade. Nevertheless for some six months in 1936 the successor to the *J.C. Madge*, the *Foresters' Centenary* was housed at the Old Hythe and launched on her first three rescue missions from there.

When Admiral of the Fleet, Lord Keyes named the *Foresters' Centenary* in July 1936 the event commanded a full page spread in *The Times* the following day. Other stations along the coast including Skegness, Wells and Cromer had received motor lifeboats several years previously and with the arrival of the *Foresters' Centenary* coverage of the North Norfolk coast by motor lifeboats was completed – just 37 months before hostilities began. From the outbreak of World War II, lifeboat work around the coast became more dangerous than ever, due to enemy action, floating mines, wrecks and various unlit navigation hazards. Efficient alternative methods for calling the crew were required as the traditional maroons were banned throughout the war. The Honorary Secretary, Mr. H.R. Johnson, used the telephone to great effect. For example, on one morning in October 1942 he made and received 21 'phone calls in 26 minutes resulting in the *Foresters' Centenary* rescuing 6 Polish airmen from a rubber dinghy. Help from the local army garrison was called on for the speedy launching of the lifeboat, as 50 to 100 men were

8

required to launch the *Foresters' Centenary* at low tide, there being no tractor at Sheringham until some years after the end of the war. On many occasions during World War II the *Foresters' Centenary* stood-by on the slipway facing the sea or even launched as a precaution when RAF and USAAF planes were returning. Aircrew flying from local airfields saw these efforts and dubbed the *Foresters' Centenary* the "Airman's Lifeboat". In gratitude, the Sheringham lifeboat crew were invited to RAF Bircham Newton aerodrome as guests of the "Kipper Patrol" which flew regularly off the coast. Sheringham lifeboat saved more airmen than any other RNLI boat, a total of 26 airmen were saved by the Sheringham lifeboat and fishing boats during World War II.

Lifeboat design altered radically after the war with petrol engines being replaced by new generations of diesel engines, along with more effective communication and navigation systems. A new design of carriage or slipway launched a 37-foot self-righting twin screw lifeboat designed by the RNLI's chief naval architect Mr. R.A. Oakley in the 1950s and the second of the class. The *Manchester Unity of Oddfellows* was allocated to Sheringham in 1961 to replace the *Foresters' Centenary*. Launching a boat off Sheringham's open beach is often risky, as little momentum is gained before hitting the first breakers. Consequently, the increased power from the twin diesel engines of the Oakley class lifeboat was appreciated very quickly at Sheringham. On launching to the converted ships lifeboat *Lucy* in August 1961 the haul-off post snapped just after the lifeboat hit the rough seas. Skilful action by the coxswain and the power from the twin engines saved the lifeboat from broaching to in the steep seas hitting the beach. Further technical developments in following decades, such as VHF radio, radio direction finding and radar, all assisted but did not replace the need for fine seamanship from the coxswains and crews as described graphically in this book. The saving of two scuba divers in September 1985 illustrates this point clearly. Only the knowledge of tidal strengths and directions combined with keen eyesight resulted in the successful rescue of the divers just before they finally succumbed to the cold.

Another revolution in lifeboat design in the late 1980s resulted in Sheringham receiving the first station lifeboat of the Atlantic 75 design. So Sheringham's tradition of life-saving is kept alive today by the town's fast inshore boat *Manchester Unity of Oddfellows*, as ready as all her predecessors to save life at sea.

Artists Preface

The story of the Sheringham lifeboats is a subject that has been close to my heart for many years. The seeds for this book were sown in the fifties on the beach, around the fishermen, watching the North sea in its many moods and hearing stories of the courage and determination of the lifeboat crews battling in the face of a North sea gale.

The *S.S. Uller* rescue where the town had no news of the *J.C. Madge* and her crew for four days, most of which was spent at sea in blizzard conditions in an open boat.

Or the service to the *Wimbledon* where mechanic Teddy 'Lux' Craske spent most of the rescue working the engines up to his armpits in water. Such bravery and selflessness under such duress is what inspires me to portray these courageous exploits.

Being involved with historical subject matter and recreating the past I am dealing with something I have not seen or experienced, only read or researched. Information on the earlier rescues is very scant, descriptions are brief and photographs of wrecks are extremely scarce, a lot is left to artistic licence and imagination.

With the more recent rescues say from the 1940s, its easier in one way! far more information is now available. On the other hand your research has to be more thorough and accuracy is essential. There are people still around that remember or were involved in the incidents and are quick to point out any errors.

I am grateful to Robin and Linda West for a great introduction and for making my task easier by allowing me to use their research and text for the majority of the descriptions in this book. Also my thanks to Henry 'Joyful' West for a fine Norfolk foreword.

I would like to think that the paintings in this book provide a unique testimony to the exploits of the Sheringham lifeboat crews over the last two centuries.

I hope you get as much satisfaction from these pictures as I did from researching and painting them.

Mick Bensley

The Augusta
Private Lifeboat 1838 – 1894

After some severe gales along the East coast in 1836 caused a number of deaths amongst the Sheringham fishermen, the Hon. Mrs. Charlotte Upcher of Sheringham Hall provided the fishing community with a lifeboat.

She was built by Robert Sunman in the style of the local crab boats, at a cost of £134.12s.2d. The lifeboat was named *Augusta* after Mrs. Upcher's youngest child, and launched on 14th November 1838. The *Augusta* measured 33'6" long and 10'3" wide, was fitted with 16 oars, a dipping-lug mainsail, standing-lug mizzen sail, and had fittings for the rudder at both ends to avoid turning her in heavy seas. Her services were not recorded at the time, and although tradition credits her with 200 launches and 1000 lives saved, research has so far established just over 200 lives saved in 16 launches, with at least a further 4 unconfirmed launches.

Coxswains of *Augusta*: Robert Long 1838–1859 and Tom Barnes Cooper 1859–1894.

THE AUGUSTA RETURNING FROM THE BRIG 'ALPHA' MAY, 1845

Dygden

5th February, 1841

The first launch where it was recorded that lives were saved has been described as a "nearly new Russian barque of 600 tons, from Abo". This casualty was the *Dygden*, laden with timber and bound from Abo to Gibraltar, which got into trouble off the town on 5th February 1841. The *Augusta* was launched into heavy seas, the waves throwing her bows skywards and all but overwhelming her. While the lifeboat was making her way towards the barque it suddenly hoisted sail, and the *Augusta* was unable to overtake her until both craft were off Blakeney. The barque's crew then pointed to Blakeney Church and explained that as they were off 'Dover Castle' they were quite safe. The Rev. Arthur Upcher related that the crew were all drunk and "had been beating about the North Sea for a fortnight without a notion of where they were". When their danger was explained the crew of the barque were eager to scramble into the lifeboat, but the captain then wished to leave the cabin boy on board to prevent claims for salvage being made. Only when the Sheringham fishermen told him "we will not take one unless we take all" did he relent, and her crew of 17 was landed at Brancaster.

Westcliff, circa 1890's

*The Augusta rounding on the Russian barque Dygden,
Feb. 1841*

Nautilus
15th April, 1845

On 15th April 1845, the Brig *Nautilus* of Aberdeen was wrecked on shore between Sheringham and Wells, in a Northerly gale. The *Augusta* took off her crew of 8 and landed them at Sheringham. The shipwrecked sailors were taken to the Crown Inn, whose landlady kept spare clothes for just such emergencies. They were given a dinner at Sheringham Hall on 17th April and so must have remained in the town for some days, hoping that it would be possible to salve their ship; but it was reported in Lloyds List that the *Nautilus* broke up on the 21st, and only some spars and materials were saved.

Tom Barnes Cooper, Coxswain of the 'Augusta' 1859-1894 and The 'Henry Ramey' 1894-1898

The Augusta alongside the brig Nautilus, April 1845

Villa Franca

14th October, 1879

The *Augusta* is credited with saving 60 lives from the barque *Villa Franca*, however this number was made up of both crew members and beachmen, who had been attempting to salvage the vessel. The *Villa Franca* was loaded with coal, and en route for Carthagena from the Tyne when she grounded at Sheringham on 13th October 1879. It was clear by the next day that she was unlikely to be got off, and her Captain employed some of the local beachmen to strip the vessel of her cargo. That evening a gale sprung up suddenly from the NNE, and the sea became so rough that it seemed likely that she would break up during the night. The *Augusta* rescued the *Villa Franca's* crew and the beachmen, and landed them at Sheringham. During the storm the barque broke her back and although the stores and rigging were later salvaged, another gale on the 18th October caused the vessel to part amidships and break up, leaving her cargo scattered on the foreshore.

*The Augusta coming alongside the barque Villa Franca,
Oct. 1879*

Alert

6th January, 1881

The service to the brig *Alert* on 6th January 1881 was brought to the notice of the RNLI, and was reported in the Lifeboat Journal. The *Alert* was a vessel of 198 tons register, and had been bound from Sunderland to Dartmouth with a cargo of coal. A NE gale had been blowing on the East Coast during the early hours of 6th January, and at daybreak watchers on the cliffs at Sheringham could see a ship in distress. The vessel had lost her mainmast and was running ashore at Cley.

The *Augusta* was launched and reached the *Alert* just ten minutes before she grounded. her seven man crew was rescued and landed at Wells Quay, while just half an hour after their rescue, the vessel had broken up and become a complete wreck.

The Augusta hauling up to the stern of the brig Alert, Jan. 1881

"Old Buck" Craske

Carolina
6th December, 1882

The Swedish barque *Carolina*, carrying coal from Hull to Trelleborg was seen anchored about two miles off Sheringham early on the 6th December 1882, having lost sails and spars. In response to signals, both the *Augusta* and the *Duncan* launched to her assistance and eventually escorted her to Grimsby, arriving just before 5pm the next day.

This was the *Duncan's* last service.

The Augusta and the Duncan on call to the Swedish barque Carolina, Dec. 1882

Services by the Augusta
1838 – 1894

7/6/1839	*Request* of South Shields	Asstd. Vessel
5/ 2/1841	Russian Barque *Dygden*	Saved 17
29/ 9/1842	Schooner *Hamburg* of Dundee	Saved 8
15/ 4/1845	Brig *Nautilus* of Aberdeen	Saved 8
21 / 5/1845	Brig *Alpha* of Shields	Saved 8
13/10/1846	Fishing Boats	Saved 81
12/ 4/1852	Crab Boats	Stood by
30/ 5/1855	The *Reformation* of Woodbridge	Saved crew
7/ 3/1864	French Lugger *Chasseur*	Saved 5
4/ 1/1865	Steam Ship *Amphion*	Landed crew
22/10/1869	*William Frothingham* of New York	Asstd. Vessel
13/10/1879	Barque *Villa Franca*	Saved 60
6/ 1/1881	Brig *Alert*	Saved 7
6/12/1882	Norwegian Barque *Carolina*	Saved crew
20/ 9/1892	Fishing Boats	Saved 11
16/ 8/1894	Fishing Boats of Sheringham	
	Brig *Gallena* of Shields	Saved 8
	Margaret Thompson of Brandsmouth	Asstd. Vessel
	An Austrian Barque	Asstd. Vessel
	Balaclava	Asstd. Vessel

The Duncan

The first RNLI Lifeboat 1867 – 1886

The RNLI organised a Branch Committee at Sheringham in 1866, and on 31st July 1867 the *Duncan* was brought to Fakenham by the Great Eastern Railway, completing the journey to Sheringham by road on her carriage.

The *Duncan* was 36' long and 9' 4" wide, she was self-righting by virtue of her heavy iron keel and high end boxes, and was supplied with 12 oars and a single mast with sail. She was built by Forrestt of Limehouse for £345, the cost being met by a donation from Mrs. Agnes Fraser (née Duncan) in memory of her father and uncle. The *Duncan* remained at Sheringham for 19 years, made 7 effective services and saved 18 lives.

Coxswains of the *Duncan*: Edmund Pye West 1867–1868, John Grice 1869, William 'Buck' Craske 1870–1873, Abraham Cooper 1874 and Robert 'Philoloo' Cooper 1875–1886.

Hero of Maldon

3rd December, 1867

The *Duncan's* first three services: to the *Hero of Maldon*, the *Frances Ann* of Goole and the *Trusty* of Boston were very similar. The first two had previously anchored off Sheringham and, finding themselves in trouble, slipped their cables and ran ashore. The *Trusty* was driven on shore at Runton by a gale and became a wreck. Each time the *Duncan* launched swiftly to the rescue, and in spite of grounding herself during the service to the *Hero* succeeded in saving three lives from each vessel. The names of the crew who went to the assistance of the *Frances Ann* were recorded in the minutes of the Local Committee; many of them from families still associated with Sheringham lifeboats over one hundred years later.

Jon Grice (senior coxswain), Edmund 'Pye' West (assistant coxswain), Rob Little, Rob John Little, Rob Bishop, Will Bishop, Thomas Ward, Robert Grice, Henry West, Joshua West, Will Hardy, Christopher Craske, George Craske, Christopher West, Robert West, Robert Woodhouse, Elmer West, James Cooper and Will Johnson.

The Duncan pulling out to the schooner Hero, Dec. 1867

Frances Ann of Goole
20th March, 1869

*The Duncan returning from service to the schooner
Frances Ann, March 1869*

Trusty of Boston
19th October, 1869

*The Duncan pulling away from the schooner Trusty,
Oct. 1869*

Wells of Goole

14th April, 1876

The schooner *Wells* of Goole was seen flying a signal of distress at dawn on 14th April 1876. She had been sailing from London to York with a cargo of superphosphate and was in a dangerous position, anchored on a lee shore. The *Duncan* launched into a heavy East gale with snow, and when lifeboatmen boarded the *Wells* at about 7am, they found she was leaking badly, had lost sails and suffered other damage during the storm. The vessel's cable was slipped, and she was taken into Holkham Bay accompanied by the lifeboat. From there she was towed into Blakeney harbour by a steamer. This service was a severe test for both lifeboat and men. Lloyd's list states that "…The lifeboatmen were exposed for many hours in the boat without provisions in a very heavy gale and tremendous sea with snow and sleet."

ABRAHAM COOPER
Coxswain: Duncan 1874-1875

The Duncan alongside the schooner Wells, April 1876

Alpha of Faversham

4th October, 1883

On 4th October 1883, the schooner *Alpha* of Faversham got into difficulties and was wrecked off Cromer. The Cromer lifeboat launched, but failed to reach the wreck and the Cromer rocket brigade was unable to make contact. A messenger was sent to Sheringham and the *Duncan* was taken on its carriage to East Runton, but she was unable to launch as the tide was too high to allow the carriage to negotiate the gangway. Eventually the vessel parted amidships and the part containing the crew drifted nearer to the shore enabling a Cromer Coastguard and two Sheringham fishermen, Edward Craske and Robert Bishop to enter the surf with lines to save the five man crew.

The rescue from the brig Alpha, Oct. 1883

Services by the Duncan
1867-1886

3/12/1867	*Hero* of Maldon	Saved 3
20/3/1869	*Frances Ann* of Goole	Saved 3
19/10/1869	*Trusty* of Boston	Saved 3
10/10/1875	*Gleaner* of Sheringham	Saved 2
14/ 4/1876	Schooner *Wells* of Goole	Asstd. to save vessel + 5
21/5/1877	Fishing boat	Saved Boat + 2
6/12/1882	Norwegian barque *Carolina*	Rendered assistance

Henry Ramey Upcher

Private Lifeboat 1894 – 1935

The *Henry Ramey Upcher* was the gift of Mrs. Caroline Upcher of Sheringham Hall, donated to the fishermen of Sheringham in memory of Mrs. Upcher's husband. She was built by Lewis "Buffalo" Emery of Sheringham, for £150, in the style of the local crab boats, using oak for the planking and fastened throughout with copper. She measured 34'9" long and 11'3" wide with a keel length of 28'9". She was double ended, carried 16 oars, and was fitted with a large dipping lug-mainsail and a mizzen. She was named by Mrs. Upcher on 4th September 1894 and remained in service until 1935; she occasionally launched for regattas until her last launch to celebrate VJ day in 1945.

Coxswains of the *Henry Ramey Upcher*:
Tom Barnes Cooper 1894–1898,
"Old Coley" Cooper 1898–1900
and Jimmy "Coley" Cooper 1900–1935.

6 Crab Boats

26th October, 1894

The weather has been very unsettled here all week, but most of the boats have managed to get out after work, although great risks were run, as there have been good catches of fish to be made. On Friday the boats went out in the morning, but shortly afterwards the swell began to come in, and fears were not groundless, for the waves increased in size at the shore, and to warn the boats at sea still became wilder, the *Henry Ramey Upcher*, the new lifeboat presented by Mrs. Upcher was launched to the rescue. At first she only acted as a guard, lying amongst the surf ready in case of accident, whilst the boats came through. On the beach willing hands, some with ropes round them in case they were drawn back with the sea, were ready to help. As soon as a boat struck she was hauled up the beach laden as it was with gear and fish. When the last half a dozen boats arrived the swell was too much for them to land, and they got on board the lifeboat and anchored their boats at sea. The lifeboat returned about quarter past five o'clock. One of the boats anchored off afterwards capsized, but very little damage was done to it. This is the first time the *Henry Ramey Upcher* has been out on service.
Taken from a local Newspaper Report of the day.

Boats getting away at dawn

*The Henry Ramey Upcher standing by fishing boats,
Oct. 1894*

Commodore
7th November, 1896

The steamer *Commodore* was driven ashore half a mile West of Sheringham, in a moderate gale on the night of 7th November 1896. Two other ships had also grounded close to the same spot earlier that day but had refloated unaided. Some of the local fishermen went to offer assistance in their own boats but shortly afterwards the wind increased and the small boats returned to shore, leaving three fishermen and the crew of fourteen men still on board. They were all rescued by the *Henry Ramey Upcher* and landed at Sheringham, at around 2am the following day. The gale continued to increase on Sunday, and by the evening the vessel was a total wreck. This wreck remained on the beach for almost seven years, until Trinity House blew it up as it was a danger to shipping.

*The Henry Ramey Upcher coming alongside the
Commodore, Nov. 1896*

Ispolen
23rd January, 1897

One of the most dramatic rescues the *Henry Ramey Upcher* undertook was to the brig Ispolen on Saturday 23rd January 1897. The *Ispolen* had run into rough weather two days previously and had shipped a lot of water; on Friday 22nd the wind rose from the NE and continued blowing all night, with thick snow squalls the following morning. The *Ispolen* made for the coast between Cromer and Sheringham on Saturday and hoping to obtain information about the nearest lifeboat station she steered for a steamer that was anchored off shore. The tide quickly drove the brig along the coast towards Sheringham and the local fishermen realised that she would soon come ashore. Both the *William Bennett* (RNLI) and the *Henry Ramey Upcher* were prepared for launching, but as the Institution slipway had been washed away in the gale the day before the *William Bennett* was taken off her carriage and dragged through the streets to the East End gangway. Meanwhile other helpers were launching the *Henry Ramey Upcher* with coxswain Barnes Cooper in charge. The *Ispolen* struck the shore at about 1.45pm, and it was soon after that the *Henry Ramey Upcher* reached the wreck. The Norwegian crew had no ropes ready when the lifeboat first made contact, and the seas swept the lifeboat onto the *Ispolen*, breaking two oars and damaging the lifeboat's cork fender. The crew nonetheless managed a second approach to the wreck, and this time threw grappling hooks into the brig's rigging and hauled the lifeboat alongside. She was held there in constant danger from the damaged masts and spars of the *Ispolen*, while the crew of 8 jumped to safety. They were soon landed at Sheringham, the news reaching the crew of the *William Bennett* just as they were about to launch. The shipwrecked sailors were taken to the Two Lifeboats Coffee Room (now the Two Lifeboats Hotel) and given hot food and dry clothes. Their ship went to pieces later that evening, leaving her cargo of ice scattered along the shore. A few ribs can still be seen on the beach beside "Upcher's breakwater" when the sand has been scoured away by the sea.

*The Henry Ramey Upcher taking the crew from the brig
Ispolen, Jan. 1897*

Teutonic and Gothic
6th January, 1906

The *J.C. Madge* carried out her first service on the 6th January 1906. While she was preparing to launch on a quarterly exercise, a vessel was seen a couple of miles to sea hoisting a distress signal. The *J.C. Madge* proceeded swiftly to the assistance of the vessel, but meanwhile a second ship was also seen in distress, with a steamer making unsuccessful attempts to help. The Sheringham fishermen at once ran to launch the *Henry Ramey Upcher*, but as it was low tide, and many fishermen were still at the Old Hythe after launching the *J.C. Madge*, it took some time to get the *Henry Ramey Upcher* afloat. The casualties were the barges *Gothic* and *Teutonic*, both owned by E.J. & W. Goldsmith. The *Gothic* had lost her headsails and bowsprit. When the *J.C. Madge* reached her the lifeboatmen assisted her crew to lay out a second anchor and she was then left to ride out the storm, while the three men on board returned to Sheringham in the lifeboat. On reaching the *Teutonic*, the private lifeboat took off her crew of four and left the vessel at anchor. That night the wind blew a gale from the NNE, which eased off towards morning. News of the barges' condition had been received at Yarmouth and at daybreak two steam tugs came to find the barges which had dragged their anchors about two miles during the gale. The barges' crews asked the lifeboatmen to return them to their vessels, since if they were unattended when the tugs arrived, salvage would be claimed. There was a race between the *Henry Ramey Upcher* and one of the tugs, but the lifeboat reached the *Teutonic* first, and then kept the tug Captains talking so that the *J.C. Madge* could reach the *Gothic*. The two masters were so pleased to get possession of their barges that they employed the lifeboatmen to assist them to Yarmouth. The two barges were towed half-way to Yarmouth by the *J.C. Madge* and the *Henry Ramey Upcher*, and then the fishermen agreed to pay the Yarmouth tugs £10 each to tow them the rest of the way. The *Gothic* and *Teutonic* arrived at Yarmouth harbour on the 8th January.

The Henry Ramey Upcher alongside the barge Teutonic, 6th Jan. 1906

*The Henry Ramey Upcher racing the tugs to the barges
Teutonic and Gothic, 7th Jan. 1906*

Empress
23rd January, 1915

Often during the first World War soldiers would assist in launching the lifeboats. One such occasion was on 23rd January 1915 when a vessel was seen firing rockets; the *Henry Ramey Upcher* was launched in 20 minutes, and the *J.C. Madge* in less than 50 minutes from its boathouse one mile west of the town having the advantage of wind, tide and speed of launching, the *Henry Ramey Upcher* reached the vessel first. It proved to be the *Empress* of Sunderland which had hit a wreck on the Sheringham Shoal and was itself sinking.

The *Empress* had broken her back and the captain and his crew soon had to take to the ship's boats. This they did within the hour and made for the *S.S. Tullochmore* of Newcastle then riding at anchor. The crew of 21 were rescued by the *Henry Ramey Upcher* and landed safely at Sheringham. The weather moderated the next day and the private lifeboat was again launched with the assistance of soldiers to take the captain of the *Empress* out to the wreck which had drifted off the shoal in the night. It had sunk a few miles off the town, in the Fairway, causing some hazard to shipping. Appeals were made through Lloyd's agent to have the wreck lit, but no record has been found of this having been done.

The Henry Ramey Upcher taking the crew of the S.S. Empress from the S.S. Tullochmore, Jan. 1915

Services by the Henry Ramey Upcher
1894–1935

Date	Vessel	Result
26/10/1894	4 fishing boats & a Hoveller	Saved 13
3/ 5/1895	6 Crab Boats	Saved 12
10/12/1895	2 Fishing Boats	Saved 4
26/ 1/1896	Fishing Boats	Saved 16
19/ 2/1896	SS *Dewdrop*	Asstd. Vessel
17/10/1896	SS *Astrid*	
7/11/1896	SS *Cavendish*	Asstd. Vessel
23/ 1/1897	SS *Commodore*	Saved 14+3 fishermen
3/ 2/1897	Brig *Ispolen*	Saved 8
26/ 2/1900	Lighters	Saved 12
29/ 5/1900	Schooner *Swan*	
2/12/1901	7 Whelk Boats	Saved 17
6/ 1/1906	Spritsail Barge *Teutonic*	Stood by
1/ 3/1908	Barque *Lodore*	Saved 4
5/ 6/1908	Fishing Boats	Saved 8
28/11/1910	Fishing Boats	Stood by
8/ 4/1911	8 Whelk Boats	Saved 16
21/ 1/1912	SS *Inca*	
3/12/1912	6 Fishing Boats	Saved 11
71 5/1913	Palling Fishing Boat *Lilian*	Saved 3
9/ 5/1913	Fishing Boat *Dove*	Saved Boat + 2
5/ 1/1914	5 Fishing Boats	Saved 11
16/11/1914	SS *Vera* of Newcastle	Launched to assist
23/ 1/1915	SS *Empress* of Sunderland	Saved 21
12/ 5/1915	5 Fishing Boats	Saved 11
26/ 4/1919	MFV *Maple Leaf*	Stood by
26/ 7/1919	MFV's *Welcome Home & Premier*	Stood by
30/ 1/1921	Whelk Boats	Stood by
12/ 2/1927	SS *Helmsman* of Newcastle	Stood by
8/ 5/1928	Crab Boats	Saved 2
18/ 2/1930	*White Heather & Welcome Home*	Saved 3
27/ 5/1932	Crab Boat *Gwendoline*	Saved 2
11/ 5/1935	9 Fishing Boats of Sheringham	Stood by

William Bennett

1886 – 1904

The *William Bennett* arrived at Sheringham on 7th July 1886, by sea. She was 41'4" long by 9'3" wide, had 14 oars and was of a self-righting design similar to the Peake type with distinctive curved washboards running along the fore and aft end-boxes. She was built by Forrestt of Limehouse and cost £500 13s 10d, paid by a legacy from Mr. W. Bennett of Regent's Park, London. The lifeboat's mast, rig and sails were designed by local fishermen and constructed in the RNLI yards in London. The *William Bennett* was just over 5 feet longer, and considerably heavier than the *Duncan*, and this combined with the narrow access to the slipway, made the *William Bennett* a very difficult boat to launch. Consequently, during the 18 years she was stationed at Sheringham, she made only four successful service launches, saving 11 lives.

Coxswains of the *William Bennett*: Robert Davidson 1886–1897 and W "Click" Bishop 1897–1904.

Fishing Boats
7th March, 1898

In March 1898 the *William Bennett* launched in a moderate ENE Gale and heavy seas, however on this occasion most of the boats were able to land while the lifeboat stood by. Only one boat had great difficulties, and her crew of two were taken into the *William Bennett*, leaving their own boat to wash ashore later in the evening.

Looking East, circa 1890's

The William Bennett on call to fishing boats, Sept. 1892

Henry Ramey Upcher
29th May, 1900

The Henry Ramey Upcher rescued 17 men from the fishing boats, and the William Bennett launched to stand by while the Henry Ramey beached as she was overloaded, May 1900

On 29th May 1900 seven whelk boats were caught 6 or 7 miles from shore by a steadily rising NNE gale and by the time they reached Sheringham conditions on the beach were too bad for them to land safely. The *Henry Ramey Upcher* took seventeen men from the fishing boats, leaving the craft to drift, but was then overloaded with around fifty men on board as she had a double crew. Signals were made for assistance from the *William Bennett* which put off and stood by while the *Henry Ramey Upcher* landed the survivors.

Asteroid
10th September, 1903

The *William Bennett's* final service, to the steam yacht *Asteroid*, was probably her most severe test. The yacht had passed Cromer on 10th September 1903 and anchored off Cley. The next day the strong southerly wind veered to the North and rose to gale force; the Blakeney lifeboat launched just before 10am, but was recalled as at that time the *Asteroid* was showing no signals of distress. While she was returning, and out of sight of the vessel, the *Asteroid* raised her ensign upside down – an international signal of distress. The Wells lifeboat had gone out of contact, a message was sent to Sheringham and the Cley lifesaving brigade. The *William Bennett* launched at 11.45am into a tremendous sea. She was double-manned, carrying a crew of thirty, because of the heavy pulling that would be required to reach Cley. She shipped a great quantity of water just after launching, and when some half mile from shore she was completely buried by an enormous sea which tore two of her oars away, but fortunately left her otherwise unscathed. She continued to row until about a mile offshore, and then lay-to while sails were hoisted before proceeding to the assistance of the *Asteroid*. It was discovered that the vessel's machinery had broken down, and so eleven lifeboatmen were put aboard to help while she was taken in tow. Pausing off Sheringham to take on supplies for the journey, the two vessels proceeded towards Yarmouth. The *Asteroid's* engineers managed to make repairs by the time they were off the Cockle lightship, and she reached the harbour under her own steam, accompanied by the lifeboat, in the early hours of the 12th. The *William Bennett* returned to her station that evening having been afloat for about twenty hours in very severe conditions.

The William Bennett on call to the Steam yacht Asteroid, Sept. 1903

Services by the William Bennett
1886-1904

20/9/1892	Fishing Boats	Saved 4
16/8/1894	Fishing Boats of Sheringham	Rendered assistance
7/3/1898	Fishing Boats of Sheringham	Stood by & Saved 2
29/ 5/1900	Launched to stand by *Henry Ramey Upcher*	
11/9/1903	Steam Yacht *Asteroid* of London	Saved 5

J.C. Madge

1904 – 1936

The *J.C. Madge* was a 41' long x 11' wide, non self-righting, pulling and sailing Liverpool class boat, the largest of the type ever built. She was rowed by 16 oars, double-banked, and had two drop-keels, two water-ballast tanks and two masts. The fore-mast carried a dipping lug-sail and the mizzen mast a standing lug-sail. She was built at the Thames Ironworks Shipbuilding Co. Ltd., Blackwall, at a cost of £1,436, provided by a legacy from Mr. James C. Madge of Southampton. She arrived on station on the 2nd December 1904, having sailed around the coast from Blackwall. The *J.C. Madge* was housed in a newly built, corrugated iron boathouse at the Old Hythe (at the western end of the Sheringham golf course) and named on the 13th December. In all, the *J.C. Madge* was launched on service 34 times, and saved 58 lives.

Coxswains of the *J.C. Madge*: William "Click" Bishop 1904–1914, Obadiah Cooper 1914–1924 and James Dumble 1924–1936.

Gothic
6th January, 1906

The *J.C. Madge* carried out her first service on the 6th January 1906. While she was preparing to launch on quarterly exercise, a vessel was seen a couple of miles to sea hoisting a distress signal. The *J.C. Madge* proceeded swiftly to the assistance of the vessel, but meanwhile a second ship was also seen in distress. The casualties were the barges *Gothic* and *Teutonic*. The *Gothic* had lost her headsails and bowsprit. When the *J.C. Madge* reached the *Gothic* the lifeboatmen assisted her crew to lay out second anchor and she was then left to ride out the storm, while the three crew returned to Sheringham in the lifeboat.
(full story page 36).

EAST BEACH, CIRCA 1890

*The J.C. Madge about to take the crew from the barge
Gothic, Jan. 1906*

Lord Moreton
24th November, 1909

The *J.C. Madge* was launched again to a barge, the *Lord Moreton*. She was seen by the Coastguard making distress signals between Cley and Blakeney on the afternoon of the 24th November 1909. The *J.C. Madge* was launched promptly, and found the barge with broken steering gear and her crew of three hands in very poor shape after battling against the severe weather in a craft that was virtually unmanageable. The lifeboatmen boarded her and rigged up a temporary rudder to steer the barge, and succeeded in assisting her to Yarmouth Roads where a tug assisted her into the harbour, accompanied by the lifeboat.

The J.C. Madge alongside the barge Lord Moreton,
Nov. 1909

S.S. Uller

24th/28th February, 1916

Early on the 24th February 1916, the *Uller* of Bergen grounded, probably on the Dudgeon Sands. She had later floated off, seriously damaged forward and leaking, and drifted for about eighteen hours before grounding again on the Blakeney Overfalls, where she remained stuck for some time before floating clear into deep water again. Reports came in that the Wells and Cromer lifeboats were unable to launch and so, in a swirling blizzard, the maroons called out the Sheringham lifeboat. The lifeboatmen's run along the cliffs was made more dangerous by the thick snow. The *J.C. Madge* was launched, with Coxswain Obadiah Cooper in charge. Owing to the strength of the wind and wild breakers it was impossible to row the boat out from the beach, so it was pulled to sea using the haul-off warp. The first wave she met as she left the carriage completely buried her and drenched her crew. Once at sea, the lifeboatmen hoisted a small storm sail and made their way towards Wells.

The J.C. Madge launching to the S.S. Uller, Feb. 1916

S.S. Uller
24th/28th February, 1916

On reaching the *Uller*, which appeared deserted with her bows submerged, the crew took the *J.C. Madge* alongside and the second coxswain and a crewman went on board. They found the *Uller's* Captain, who decided that as he had half steam, he would try to keep his vessel afloat. So at the Captain's request the open lifeboat and her crew stood by the *Uller* all night in appalling conditions. In the morning the *Uller* began to make her way towards Grimsby, at half speed, with all pumps working. The lifeboat swung at the end of a 90ft tow, every sea threatening to lift the craft and smash her onto the *Uller's* propeller which was half out of the water. It was to be a race against time, as the Grimsby boom defences would be closed at sunset, and there were some 53 miles to be covered. Once the two vessels reached the Humber, a pilot came out and it was decided that nothing could be done for the *Uller* at Grimsby. With some reluctance, the pilot took her on to King George dock, Hull, while the lifeboatmen spent the night at Grimsby with friends and relatives. When the two craft had arrived in the Humber, a Government ship had enquired which station the lifeboat was from, and it was believed that a message had then been passed on to Sheringham, so although the storm had brought down telephone lines, the crew did not worry about their families at home. The following day the Sheringham Lifeboat was called to stand by a ship that had gone ashore at Spurn Point, but on this occasion no help was required and the lifeboatmen made the long journey home with assistance from a French steamer. The *J.C. Madge* eventually arrived back at her station at about 6pm on the 28th February. The relief felt by the families and friends of the crewmen can only be imagined, because no message had been received about the lifeboat since she had left her carriage and headed into the raging seas four days before.

OBADIAH COOPER
Coxswain: J.C. Madge 1914–1924

The J.C. Madge being towed by the S.S. Uller, Feb. 1916

Ingeborg
15th November, 1925

The *J.C. Madge* launched to the *Ingeborg*, a fine four-masted schooner, with 160hp auxiliary motors, on 15th November 1925. While on a voyage from Oskarshamm, Sweden to Plymouth with a cargo of timber and a crew of ten, she ran ashore at Spallow Gap. It was found that she was aground by the bows in a little over seven feet of water. Anchors were laid out and tugs requested from Yarmouth. At about 6.30pm she was towed astern into deep water, breaking the two anchor cables as she did so. Tugs proceeded to tow the *Ingeborg* to Yarmouth accompanied by the lifeboat. Two Yarmouth tugs, the *Yare* and the *George Jewson* and three local fishing boats (*Welcome Home, Little May and Sunbeam*) were employed, along with the *J.C. Madge* which had assisted to save the ten crewmen. The *Ingeborg* had been at Oskarshamm for temporary repairs, after having stranded at Berqvara the month before.

*The J.C. Madge standing by as the tugs attempt to tow off
the stranded Ingeborg, Nov. 1925*

Services by the J.C. Madge
1904-1936

6/1/1906	Barge *Gothic* of London	Saved 3
71 1/1906	Barge *Gothic* of London	Asstd. to save barge
24-25/11/09	Barge *Lord Moreton* of London	Saved boat + 3
8/ 4/1911	Fishing Boats of Sheringham	Saved 4 boats + 12
24/2/1916	SS *Uller* of Bergen	Saved 3
16/3/1916	SS *Rhenania* CT5	Asstd. save boat + 7
18/4/1918	Collier *Alice Taylor* of Dundee	Saved 18
9/2/1924	Barge *Oceanic* of London	Asstd. save boat + 3
15/11/1925	Schooner *Ingeborg* of Helsingborg	Asstd. save boat + 10
12/ 2/1927	SS *Helmsman* of Newcastle	Stood by
3/1/1930	SS *Lestris* of Bruges	Gave assistance
13/12/1933	Barge *Fred Everard* of Blakeney	Stood by
31/5/1935	Schooner *Six Sisters* of Hull	Gave assistance
2/ 4/1936	WPB *Little Madge* of Sheringham	Saved Boat + 2
16/11/1914	SS *Vera*	
23/ 1/1915	SS *Empress*	Asstd. save vessel
26/12/1917	To assistance of unknown steamer in distress	
5/ 3/1918	SS *Unbeknown*	To assist vessel & crew
5/4/1918	2 French FVs wrecked off Blakeney	To assist vessels & crew
15/ 7/1919	To assistance of crew of HM Airship 11 on fire	
5/ 1/1921	To assistance of SS *Glencain* which declined help	
12/ 1/1922	To assistance of unknown steamer	
2/ 6/1922	In response to wireless message, launched to assistance of 2 steamers reported in collision off the Dudgeon LV, but failed to find them	

Foresters' Centenary
1936 – 1961

The *Foresters' Centenary* was a 35'6" long x 10'3" wide single screw, non self-righting Liverpool class motor lifeboat built in 1936 at Groves & Guttridge, Isle of Wight, at a cost of £3,569. She was fitted with one 35hp petrol engine, designed by the RNLI and built by Weyburn of Surrey, which gave her a maximum speed of 7.3 knots and a cruising speed of 6.3 knots. She was also supplied with jib, main and mizzen sails as back-up in case of engine failure. She was the fifth boat donated to the RNLI by the Ancient Order of Foresters' Friendly Society and while at Sheringham she launched on service 129 times saving 82 lives, more than any other Foresters' lifeboat up to that time.

Coxswains of the *Foresters' Centenary*:
James Dumble 1936–1947,
Sparrow Hardingham 1947–1950
and Henry "Downtide" West 1951–1961.

Boston Trader
9th February, 1940

On the 9th February, 1940 *Foresters' Centenary* was called out to save life after a German aircraft had attacked the coaster *Boston Trader*, and set her on fire about three miles off Cley. The Hon. Sec. was informed, and the lifeboat was launched only eighteen minutes after the attack, in spite of having to be dragged over the sand. The weather was thick, and the sea rough with half a gale blowing from the East. Cley Coastguard continued to watch the vessel, and at 1pm a small boat was seen leaving the ship. It was feared that she would capsize when approaching the shore, but the lifeboat crew also saw the boat, and as they were afraid for her safety too, they raised a sail to signal that they were on their way. The *Boston Trader's* crew held their boat off shore, and when they were taken in to the lifeboat there were only a few inches of their small boat above water, and it sank shortly after. The lifeboat went to the coaster, but found that she was so completely on fire that nothing could be done to save her. Her seven crew were landed at Sheringham at 3.25pm and the wounded attended to. *Boston Trader* later drifted ashore on Blakeney Point, the rough seas put out the fire and she was later salvaged. The Captain of the *Boston Trader* pointed out in his letter of thanks, that had the Sheringham crew not been so prompt in getting to them, their boat would probably have been driven ashore and all of her occupants drowned.

JAMES DUMBLE
Coxswain: J.C. Madgo 1924-1936 and Foresters' Centenary 1936-1947

The Foresters' Centenary on call to fishing boats

*The Foresters' Centenary picking up the survivors from the
bombed Boston Trader, Feb. 1940*

Czajk

6th November, 1954

A trawler from the Polish fishing fleet, the *Czajk* of Swinoujscie, ran aground in calm conditions, off Beeston Hill at about 3am on 6th November 1954. She was discovered at 6.30am and the *Foresters' Centenary* was launched into a calm sea with drizzle falling but with the wind begining to strengthen from the North East. The lifeboat stood by the trawler for most of the day, with the second coxswain Mr. Henry "Joyful" West going on board twice to explain to the crew that the weather was deteriorating and offering lifeboat assistance in laying out double anchors. All offers of help were refused, including those from the Gt. Yarmouth tug *Richard Lee Barber*. Three of the trawler's sister ships stood by and one tried to refloat her on the afternoon high tide but this attempt was abandoned after the tow rope snapped. Five crew transferred by small boat to a sister ship. The *Foresters' Centenary* returned station at 5.35pm that night as rescue attempts were halted until the following morning. The *Foresters' Centenary* re-launched at noon the next day to assist the tug to attach a towing hawser to the *Czajk* of Swinoujscie. This was achieved despite the lifeboat having to work amongst the rocks and dangerous rollers and would have been much easier the previous afternoon when the offer was first made.

Henry "Downtide" West
Coxswain of Foresters Centenary 1951-1961 and the Manchester Unity of Oddfellows 1961-1962

*The Foresters' Centenary standing by while the tug
Richard Lee Barber attempts to tow off the Polish Trawler
Czajk, Nov. 1954*

Gold

8th/9th December, 1954

A few weeks later, two services were made to the barge *Gold*, again under difficult conditions. These highlighted the limitations of the petrol-engined single screw Liverpool type lifeboats and resulted in a campaign for a boat with more power to be placed at Sheringham. Red flares were sighted off Weybourne on 8th December 1954 and a "Mayday" radio message was heard by the station Hon. Sec., from the *SS Rota*, reporting that a motor barge was near the shore between Blakeney Point and Sheringham firing red rockets. The *Foresters' Centenary* was prepared for launching down the slipway but had to be returned to the level turntable to hand start the engine. On launching, the lifeboat went alongside the *SS Rota* which had taken off the two man crew from the barge *Gold* of Rochester. The two men were transferred to the lifeboat and due to their state of exhaustion landed at Sheringham. The barge had been anchored but was in great danger of blowing ashore. Consequently, the *Foresters' Centenary* was re-launched just after midnight to tow the vessel to safety. The casualty was rolling and pitching violently close to the shore and so low in the water that her decks were continuously awash. Two lifeboatmen, second coxswain Mr. Henry "Joyful" West and the bowman Mr. Arthur Scotter jumped onto the barge. Ropes were attached from the lifeboat which began to tow the craft towards the nearest suitable harbour at Wells. By 2.00 am, just off Blakeney Point, the tide had turned East, against them, and was so strong so that no progress was being made. Under these conditions, the lifeboatmen on the barge were barely able to keep her from broaching to. The Wells lifeboat *Cecil Paine*, a diesel twin-screw Liverpool type lifeboat was launched to assist the rescue operation and enabled the barge to be brought to anchor in Holkham Bay, west of Wells. There was sufficient depth of water to enter the harbour by 8.30am and the two lifeboats brought the barge safely to the quay.

Henry 'Joyful' West
coxswain: Manchester Unity of Oddfellows 1963-1984

The Foresters' Centenary on call to the motor barge Gold,
Dec. 1954

Zor
18th May, 1955

In May, *Foresters' Centenary* rescued four men from the *SS Zor* of Istanbul just before the cargo ship sank. The *Zor* had suffered a shift in her cargo of timber off the Norfolk coast, and five men had been rescued from her by the Wells lifeboat on the 18th May 1955. Four men had decided to remain on board the listing steamer and so the Hon. Sec. at Sheringham authorised the launch of the *Foresters' Centenary*.

The Lifeboat left the slipway through a heavy on-shore swell. As the lifeboat got further out, the weather deteriorated rapidly and at the Sheringham Shoal the sea was so rough that the coxswain decided not to risk crossing it but altered course to pass around the sand banks. Beyond the shoal, the weather continued to worsen so that the lifeboat's speed had to be reduced, to avoid losing crew men overboard.

The *Foresters' Centenary* reached the casualty 4 miles WNW of the Dudgeon Lightvessel at 6am on 19th May and it was evident to the lifeboatmen that the *Zor* was sinking. The lifeboat approached the listing vessel's starboard side to recommend that the captain and his remaining crew should abandon ship, however the captain refused. The lifeboat crew were informed that the tug *Serviceman*, was hoping to tow the *Zor* when the weather moderated, however Coxswain "Downtide" West considered that the *Zor* would sink first. The lifeboat stood by the casualty amongst the tons of timber that the sea was washing from the *Zor's* decks. The tug attached a line to the *Zor* by 8.30 am but as soon as she began to tow, the *Zor's* list increased and her condition became so critical, that her Master beckoned to the lifeboat for assistance. The ship's position had become desperate as access to the sheltered starboard side of the ship was impossible due to the amount of loose timber floating about. A rope was hanging down the exposed port side of the *Zor* so coxswain West steered the lifeboat in to ram the ship's side, and held her there with her engine while the ship's crew slid down and were hauled into the lifeboat. The *Foresters' Centenary* sheered away and informed the tug that all the crew had been saved. Less than ten minutes after the crew had been rescued the deck cargo from the *Zor* shot off and the vessel sank stern first.

The *Foresters' Centenary* arrived back at Sheringham with the four rescued survivors at 1.35pm. after a very arduous 14 hour service. This rescue earned the Thanks of the RNLI on Vellum for Coxswain Henry "Downtide" West.

THE 'GAIA' BEING TOWED IN BY THE 'FORESTER'S CENTENARY', 1950. THE YACHT HAD BEEN IN DISTRESS 25 MILES FROM SHERINGHAM

*The Foresters' Centenary taking the crew from the listing
Zor, May 1955*

S.S. Wimbledon
31st October, 1956

The most dramatic post-war rescue by the *Foresters' Centenary* was to save the crew of the *S.S. Wimbledon* on the 31st October 1956. A message was received from the Coastguard at 8.25am that the steam collier *Wimbledon* (1,598 tons) was taking in water about 13 miles NW of Cromer and requested assistance. The *S.S. Sydenham* confirmed that she was going to her aid and two other ships, the *Blythe* and *Eleanor Brook* were also standing by. Eight minutes later the *Wimbledon* radioed that her pumps could not control the rising water level and that she planned to beach at Blakeney. The Sheringham lifeboat crew were placed on standby immediately but only ten minutes later, the Mate of the *Wimbledon* reported that her Master had been washed overboard. The Master's body was picked up subsequently by the *Eleanor Brook*. The *Foresters' Centenary* was launched at 9.03am into a very rough sea and headed for the casualty, about 4 miles NE of Blakeney at about 10.15am. Meanwhile a helicopter, working beyond its normal operating conditions transferred a doctor to the *Eleanor Brook* to attend to the body of the Master of the *Wimbledon*, who he pronounced as dead.

On arrival at the *Wimbledon* the *Foresters' Centenary* transferred eight of the casualty's eighteen crew to the *Blythe* as the coxswain did not wish to risk their lives in subsequent approaches to the casualty.

Coxswain West radioed that the lifeboat's fuel supply was running low and the Wells Lifeboat was launched to assist in supplying petrol and to pick up the doctor and body from the *Eleanor Brook*. By 1.00pm the *Wimbledon* was settling

FORESTER'S CENTENARY TRANSFERRING SOME OF THE WIMBLEDON'S CREW TO THE BLYTHE

The Foresters' Centenary alongside the Wimbledon,
Oct. 1956

S.S. Wimbledon
31st October, 1956

lower in the water with seas washing over the vessel up to her bridge. Coxswain West asked the *Eleanor Brook* to persuade the Mate of the *Wimbledon* to abandon ship before it was too late. Nearly one hour elapsed before the Mate decided to do so and by this time there was a full flood tide and no shelter on either side of the ship from the force 8 NE gale blowing. With only the aft part of the *Wimbledon* above water, the coxswain steered the *Foresters' Centenary* alongside, ropes were attached and two of the crew were rescued, one of whom had sustained a head injury. The ropes snapped and again the lifeboat approached and made fast with new ropes and rescued a further two men, before the ropes broke. Three men were rescued on the third attempt before the ropes snapped and the lifeboat was swept away. By this stage no ropes could withstand the power of the sea and the coxswain was forced to drive the lifeboat onto the submerged deck of the *Wimbledon* and hold her in position with her single 35hp engine. The lifeboat motor mechanic continued to work the engine controls under the small canopy as required by the coxswain even though he was often up to his armpits in water. On this last approach, in which 2 metres of the lifeboat's port fender were ripped off, the last three men were rescued. When the lifeboat slid off the casualty only the *Wimbledon's* funnel and part of the stern were above water, and shortly after the vessel sank completely. The Mate and three of the crew were transferred to the *Sydenham* but the remaining six survivors on the *Foresters' Centenary* were so exhausted that they asked to be landed as soon as possible. The sea conditions at Sheringham were too poor for the lifeboat to return, especially since it would be dark before they arrived, so the lifeboat set course for Wells harbour which was reached by 4pm, and the remaining survivors from the *Wimbledon* were landed.

The *Foresters' Centenary* returned to Sheringham four days later when the weather conditions had improved and the damage sustained by the lifeboat during the rescue could be repaired.

For the rescue of the eighteen men from the *Wimbledon* Coxswain H.E. "Downtide" West was awarded the RNLI's Silver Medal and Motor Mechanic E.C. Craske the Bronze Medal. The RNLI's Thanks on Vellum were awarded to H. Bishop, A. Scotter, J.H. Bishop, D. Little, S. Little and R. West. Coxswain Henry "Downtide" West and Coxswain Douglas Grant of Selsey, West Sussex were the first co-recipients of awards from the James Bower Endowment Fund, established by P & O in 1955, to RNLI gold and silver medal winners. Both the silver medal rescues at Sheringham and Selsey resulted each in eighteen lives being saved.

TEDDY 'LUX' CRASKE fisherman, lifeboat mechanic and winchman

*The Foresters' Centenary snatching the last man
from the sinking Wimbledon, Oct. 1956*

Windsor Rose
24th September, 1957

On 24th September, 1957 two lives were saved from the fishing boat *Windsor Rose*. The launch was requested by Cromer No.1 lifeboat which was at sea assisting local fishing boats. The Sheringham lifeboat was launched into a rough sea just at sunset. *Foresters' Centenary* came up with *Windsor Rose* about 1 mile north of Cromer, her crew were wearing lifejackets passed to them by the Cromer lifeboat, but because of the heavy seas the fishing boat was barely under control and in imminent danger of capsizing. The lifeboat took the two men off with some difficulty and towed the boat to Sheringham. They stood off the beach for about two hours by which time conditions had improved sufficiently to allow the boats to beach.

Launching into a heavy swell with the quant

The Foresters' Centenary on call to fishing boat Windsor Rose, Sept. 1957

Services by the Foresters' Centenary 1936-1961

Date	Vessel	Service
7/8/1936	FBts. *Liberty II & Edna* of Sheringham	Escorted Bts.
19/8/1936	Small boat of West Runton	Saved boat + 1
20/9/1936	MV *Karanan* of Rotterdam	Stood by boat
7/8/1938	MV *John M* of London	Stood by boat
22/4/1939	F.Bt. *Reliance* II	Escorted boat
27/4/1939	F.Bt. *Olive* of Sheringham	Escorted boat
9/2/1940	SS *Boston Trader* of Gt Yarmouth	Saved 7
1/3/1940	SS *Jevington Court* of London	Saved ship's boat
2/3/1940	Salved a buoy	
22/4/1940	Barge *Mahelah* of London	Saved 4
1/9/1940	Aeroplane	Salved wreckage & gear
21/10/1940	A British Bomber	Saved 5
5/4/1941	Fishing boat of Sheringham	Saved boat + 3
27/10/1941	An aeroplane's dinghy	Saved 5
29/10/1941	SS *Eaglescliffe Hall* of Montreal	Saved 15
1/2/1942	Aeroplane	Salved wreckage
15/3/1942	HMS *Vortigern*	Picked up a body
30/7/1942	Aeroplane	Picked up a body
17/10/1942	Sick man on HM Trawler 677	Landed sick man
30/10/1942	Aeroplane in sea	Saved 6
13/5/1943	Aeroplane	Picked up a body
24/8/1943	F.Bt *Our Need* of Lowestoft	Gave help
17/9/1944	Admiralty MV No. 649	Gave help
24/9/1944	Fishing boats of Sheringham	Saved boats
3/4/1945	Fishing boat *Gwendoline*	Gave help
16/8/1945	Private LB *Henry Ramey Upcher*	Gave help
9/12/1945	SS *Lady Sophia*	Gave help
24/5/1946	3 fishing boats	Escorted boats
10/12/1946	MV *Bilsdale* of Middlesbrough	Escorted vessel
14/9/1947	SS *El Morro* of Portland, Oregon	Stood by
21/9/1947	Auxiliary ketch *Livre* of Burnham	Saved boat + 2
6/2/1948	3 fishing boats of Sheringham	Escorted boats
22/4/1949	6 fishing boats of Sheringham	Gave help
3-4/5/1949	SS *Barren Hill* of Panama	Stood by
11/9/1950	Steam Yacht *Gaia*	Saved boat + 4
22/9/1950	Steam Yacht *Miranda*	Saved boat + 2
31/12/1950	*Johanna Te Velde* of Holland	Gave help
7/5/1951	4 fishing boats of Sheringham	Escorted boats
27/8/1951	Dinghy *Meringue*	Saved 2
29/6/1953	3 Fishing boats	Escorted boats
6-7/11/1954	Trawler *Czajk* of Swinoujscie, Poland	Gave help
8/12/1954	MV *Gold* of Rochester	Landed two
9/12/1954	MV *Gold* of Rochester	Saved boat
18-19/5/55	SS *Zor* of Istanbul	Saved 4
2/12/1955	Motor Yacht *Flashing Stream*	Gave help
8/6/1956	4 Fishing boats	Escorted boats
31/10/1956	SS *Wimbledon*	Saved 18
29/7/1957	MY *Vanessa* of Rochester	Saved yacht + 3
30/7/1957	Fishing boat *Boy Charlie* of Hemsby	Gave help
20/8/1957	MV *Sunwood*	Saved boat + 5
24/9/1957	Fishing boat *Winsor Rose*	Saved boat + 2
31/5/1958	Sick Man on Dudgeon LV	Landed sick man
17/4/1959	3 Fishing boats	Escorted boats
26/6/1959	Yacht *Pleasant Mirth*	Gave help
16/4/1960	Fishing boat *Windsor Rose*	Gave help
16/6/1960	Yacht *Sulaipe* of Ipswich	Gave help landed 3
11/8/1960	FV *Enterprise* of Sheringham	Gave help

The Manchester Unity of Oddfellows

1961 – 1990

The *Manchester Unity of Oddfellows*, Sheringham's longest serving offshore motor lifeboat, was a 37' by 11' 6" wide, twin screw, Oakley class self-righting lifeboat. A gift of The Unity Friendly Society (The Oddfellows), she was built at William Osborne's shipyard, Littlehampton and cost £28,500. During her twenty-nine years on station at Sheringham, *The Manchester Unity of Oddfellows* launched on service 127 times and saved 134 lives.

Coxswains of *The Manchester Unity of Oddfellows*:
Henry "Downtide" West 1961–1962,
Henry "Joyful" West 1963–1984,
Jack West 1985–1986,
Brian Pegg 1986–1989
and Clive Rayment 1989–1990.

Lucy

15th August, 1961

The 15th August was more like autumn than summer; the wind was blowing strongly from the NW, whipping up a short steep sea. The converted ship's lifeboat *Lucy* was making her maiden voyage to Southwold with two men, a woman and an eleven year old boy on board. Around noon, with the weather deteriorating, they discovered that the boat had sprung a leak astern; the two men desperately began to bale. The owner's wife had taken to her bunk suffering from seasickness, while the boy remained on deck with the two men. When the owner managed to snatch a moment to see his wife, he discovered her on the cabin floor unconscious. The two men brought her out into the fresh air, but could not leave their task of baling long enough to attend to her. Their flares had become waterlogged so they collected clothes, covers and anything else that was dry and made a small fire to signal their distress. The signal was seen by the coxswain's son Mr. David West, and the new Sheringham lifeboat was launched at 1.43pm, the tide being on the slipway. With the strong North wind, it was necessary to use the haul-off rope to hold the boat's bow straight and prevent her being washed broadside onto the beach. The launch proceeded well until the boat had just left her carriage, at which point the 10ft. post on the shore, holding the haul-off rope, snapped, leaving the lifeboat at the mercy of the wind and waves. By skilful handling, Coxswain "Downtide" West managed to keep her heading out to sea and in a few moments the danger was past and *The Manchester Unity of Oddfellows* made all speed towards the *Lucy's* position. Three of the lifeboatmen were chosen to board the stricken craft: Mr. Henry "Joyful" West, Mr. Eric Wink and Mr. Arthur Scotter. Waves of between eight and ten feet high were adding to the difficulties, and it took three attempts before all three men had transferred to the *Lucy*. The woman, still unconscious, was taken into the lifeboat on the next approach, and the boy and the owner transferred to the lifeboat on the fifth run in. The lifeboat then attempted to pass a tow line to the *Lucy*, but as soon as it was made fast, the rope snapped. The fierce swell had already almost capsized the *Lucy* twice, and the lives of the remaining crew member and the three lifeboatmen on board were now in even greater peril. *The Manchester Unity of Oddfellows* made one more approach to the wreck, and in those few seconds all four men managed to scramble onto her heaving deck. The casualties were landed at Sheringham where a doctor and ambulance were waiting to attend the survivors.

The lifeboat was not rehoused, as the *Lucy* had been left drifting in the navigation channel and could have posed a danger to other shipping.

One more drama occurred. To relaunch the lifeboat, she had to be hauled back onto her carriage which had been left at the top of the slope after her first launch. As the five-ton carriage was being lowered down the ramp, it began to gather speed and the men on the ropes were unable to control it. The carriage rumbled down the slipway straight for the lifeboat. Mr. Arnold Culley, one of the local fishermen, who was holding onto a steering handle at the rear of the carriage was forced to break into a run but still managed to hang on, and hold it on a straight course, preventing it running off the slipway and possibly crushing some of the many spectators. The carriage was travelling at some 20miles an hour when it reached the beach and for a moment it seemed as if it would ram the new lifeboat, but Mr. Culley wrenched at the handle and the carriage swung clear of her.

The *Lucy* was found inside the shipping lanes, and finally washed ashore and wrecked at Salthouse. For their efforts Coxswain "Downtide" West and the three lifeboatmen who boarded the *Lucy* were awarded the Thanks of the Institution on Vellum.

Arthur Scotter, Fisherman and lifeboatman

The Manchester Unity of Oddfellows alongside the converted ship's lifeboat Lucy, Aug. 1961

S.S. Richmond Castle

9th February, 1969

On 9th February 1969, in a force 8 NE gale, *The Manchester Unity of Oddfellows* launched into darkness and driving snow to land a sick seaman from the *SS Richmond Castle*. Transferring from one vessel to another at sea is no easy matter, especially at night and in a storm, and with the very different sizes of the two vessels involved. The sick man was the Third Officer of the 800 ton vessel owned by Cayzer Irvine & Co. The lifeboat maroons were fired at 12.40am and the lifeboat made rendezvous with the steamer inside the Sheringham Shoal at 1.50am. The casualty was transferred safely and landed back at Sheringham just before 3am. He was taken by ambulance to Cromer Hospital and subsequently recovered completely and returned to work. He was very grateful for the lifeboat's assistance, and presented the station with a plaque to record the occasion.

The Manchester Unity of Oddfellows on call to the Richmond Castle, 1969

*The Manchester Unity of Oddfellows launching to the
Richmond Castle, Feb. 1969*

Sallie

6th April, 1973

On the 6th April 1973, a 44ft yacht was observed passing Sheringham; force nine NW gales were forecast and the seas were already very heavy. The Hon. Sec. called the yacht by Morse lamp to enquire if all was well but received no reply, and as darkness fell no navigation lights appeared on the boat. The yacht was close to the shore with an on-shore wind and it was established that she was the East Coast fishing smack *Sallie* on a Coastguard-surveyed passage from Lowestoft to Bridlington. The Hon. Sec. requested a Coastguard watch along the coast to the westward and at 11pm red flares were sighted 1-2 miles off Cley lookout. The lifeboat was launched and made contact with the casualty, with the aid of parachute flares, at 12.30am on the 7th. The vessel was helpless with a jammed rudder and a damaged generator; two crew members were taken off in very rough seas and the third followed after a tow line had been secured. An attempt was made to tow her closer to the beach before casting her adrift, but her jammed rudder and the rough seas combined to make the smack yaw badly, and the Samson post was pulled out of the casualty's deck. A second attempt with a grappling iron also failed because its flukes were forced straight. Owing to the deteriorating conditions the lifeboat returned to station with the three rescued crewmen, leaving the *Sallie* adrift 1 mile WNW of Blakeney Point. The craft was eventually salvaged.

*The Manchester Unity of Oddfellows coming alongside
the smack Sallie, April 1973*

Harvester and Concorde II

16th April, 1979

In April 1979, there was a tragic loss of life off Blakeney Point. While fishing off the coast the fishing vessel *Harvester* of Blakeney called her companion boat *Concorde II* on the radio but received no reply. Lifeboat bowman, Mr. Jack West, contacted *Harvester* by radio and was told that she was anchored off Weybourne and unable to start her engine. The wind was NNW force 5-6 and so the information was passed to the coxswain who kept both vessels under observation. Two and a half hours later the FV *Concorde II* informed Coastguards that she had *Harvester* in tow and was heading for Blakeney. Just after 7pm the Hon. Sec. spoke to the Blakeney Pilot who recommended that the lifeboat should be launched to escort the two boats as Blakeney harbour entrance would be extremely treacherous in the seas that were then running. The Sheringham lifeboat launched immediately and took over the tow of the *Harvester* and transferred the *Harvester's* crew into the lifeboat. Conditions at the entrance to Blakeney harbour were very bad and the lifeboat coxswain recommended that the crew of the *Concorde II* should also transfer to *The Manchester Unity Of Oddfellows*. The skipper of the fishing boat refused the offer and said that he would make his own way in. As the lifeboat was crossing the bar with *Harvester* in tow she was struck by three heavy seas in quick succession. These were so violent that they caused the lifeboat capsize warning light to be triggered. Also, between the second and third wave it was discovered that there were no lights visible from *Concorde II* and it appeared that she had been completely overwhelmed by the same waves that hit the lifeboat. Despite the confused seas in the narrow channel, the coxswain at once turned lifeboat and tow by 180 degrees and fired a flare to assist in the search for *Concorde II*. Wells lifeboat launched to assist and both boats were in the area for over four hours until the search for the boat and her crew was abandoned.

*The Manchester Unity of Oddfellows with the
Harvester under tow, April 1979*

Force Four GT
20th April, 1985

AN NE force eight gale swept down on 20th April 1985, and a 14.5 ft rigid hull inflatable, *Force Four GT*, was on its way to Brancaster watched by the Coastguards. A sudden blockage in a fuel tank left the small boat at the mercy of the steadily worsening conditions. The London couple on board were spotted waving and within 13 minutes of the call being received from the Coastguards *The Manchester Unity Of Oddfellows* was afloat and on her way. Coxswain Jack West headed towards the vessel's last reported position and after battling with the heavy seas for over an hour reached *Force Four GT* at 7.48pm. Her two occupants were taken into the lifeboat and the inflatable was towed back to Sheringham and left moored off shore. The high tide and heavy swell made it impossible to beach the lifeboat until conditions improved so *The Manchester Unity Of Oddfellows* stood off shore for an hour and a half until it was possible to land.

Jack West, Coxswain of the Manchester Unity of Oddfellows 1985-1986

*The Manchester Unity of Oddfellows on call to
Force 4 GT, April 1985*

Tor Gothia
15th February, 1989

Just after midnight on the 15th February 1989, the Hon. Sec. was informed by the Coastguard that Cromer lifeboat, which was standing by the cargo ship *Tor Gothia* aground on the Haisborough Sands, had requested assistance from the Sheringham lifeboat. At 1.20 am, the *The Manchester Unity Of Oddfellows* was launched and reached the casualty, which was aground in the middle of the Haisborough Sands, at about 3.10 am. The seas were very confused, and the shallow water over the sands was extremely rough. Shortly after *The Manchester Unity Of Oddfellows* arrived at the scene, the Cromer lifeboat left for Gt.Yarmouth. Sheringham lifeboat remained with the *Tor Gothia* and provided depth soundings around the casualty until she floated off the bank under her own steam at noon. The lifeboat arrived back at Sheringham at 3.32pm, having been at sea for over 12 hours.

Brian Pegg, BEM. Coxswain of the Manchester Unity of Oddfellows 1986-1989

*The Manchester Unity of Oddfellows on service to
the Tor Gothia, Feb. 1989*

Services by the
Manchester Unity of Oddfellows
1961-1996

Date	Vessel	Service
13/7/1961	4 Crab boats	Escorted boats
9/8/1961	Small yacht	Saved boat + 3
15/8/1961	Converted ship's lifeboat *Lucy*	Saved 4
9/7/1962	Converted ship's lifeboat *Sea Hawk*	Saved boat + 4
7/8/1962	FV *Sprat*	Saved boat + 2
15/8/1963	Cabin Cruiser *Buccaneer*	Saved boat + 3
21/8/1963	Yacht *Mona* of Scarborough	Saved boat + 2
1/9/1964	Crab boat *White Rose*	Saved boat + 2
20/6/1965	Speedboat *Sea Sprite*	Saved boat + 2
15/8/1965	Speedboat	Landed 2
5/9/1965	Motor Cruiser *Sirius* of Leith	Gave help
21/12/1965	Crab boat *Welcome Messenger*	Gave help
8/4/1966	4 Fishing boats of Sheringham	Escorted boats
1/7/1966	MV *Pantarali*	Landed 2 and a body
18/4/1967	Crab boats	Gave help
29/1/1968	Motor Cruiser *Hilary Anne*	Saved boat + 1
20/5/1968	9 Fishing boats	Escorted boats
15/5/1968	Fishing boat *Tania*	Saved boat + 2
30/6/1968	Cabin cruiser *She's a Lady*	Saved 3; Asst. to save boat
17/8/1968	Dinghy	Saved boat + 2
9/2/1969	MV *Richmond Castle*	Landed a sick man
171 9/1969	Crab boat *Cicely Elizabeth*	Escorted boat
3/1/1971	Fishing boat *Our Boys*	Escorted boat
8/2/1971	Fishing boat *Welcome Messenger*	Escorted boat
29/4/1971	8 Fishing boats	Stood by
3/6/1971	Fishing bts. *Our boys* & *Mizpah*	Stood by
9/6/1971	MFV *Peggy* of Copenhagen	Saved boat + 1
19/6/1971	*John Kay*	Saved boat + 6
6/11/1971	MFV *Nauru* of Anstruther	Saved boat + 2
31/7/1972	Cabin cruiser *Sylvia*	Gave help
16/9/1972	Yacht *Sea Boots*	Saved boat + 2
1/1/1973	Sick man on *Dudgeon* LV	Landed sick man
6/4/1973	Yacht *Sallie* of Makjon	Saved 3
24/4/1973	Sick man on *Dudgeon* LV	Landed sick man
8/8/1973	FV *Ame* of King's Lynn	Gave help
7/11/1973	Sick man on Haisborough LV	Landed sick man
27/4/1974	6 Motor fishing boats	Escorted vessels
25/11/1974	Injured man on MFV *Kilsyth*	Landed injured man
1/1/1975	Injured man on *Finnlark* of Finland	Landed injured man
2/6/1976	Yacht *Blue Tit*	Saved boat + 2
4/9/1976	Barge *Focena*	Saved boat + 2
14/11/1976	*Restless Wave*	Gave help
11/1/1977	Fishing bt. *Sea Green* of E.Runton	Escorted boat
9/7/1977	5 Fishing boats	Escorted boats
5/8/1977	Yacht *Niord*	Gave help
25/10/1977	Dinghy	Escorted boat
28/3/1978	Fishing bt. *Jonathan James*	Gave help
5/7/1978	Converted Admiralty Supply Vessel VIC 32	Escorted vessel
8/9/1978	Motor launch *Ailsa*	Gave help
29/1/1979	Fishing boat *Mizpah*	Gave help
5/4/1979	Fishing boat *Mizpah*	Escorted boat
16/4/1979	Fishing boat *Harvester*	Saved 2
26/8/1979	Motor cruiser *Dora Lee*	Saved 5
8/4/1980	Fishing boats	Escorted boats
1/5/1981	Fishing bt. *Cicely Elizabeth*	Gave help
14/7/1981	Fishing bt. *Sea Security*	Landed 3
14/7/1981	Fishing boat	Escorted boat
22/8/1981	Fishing boats	Escorted boats
6/4/1982	Motor cruiser *Lagona*	Gave help
9/8/1983	Cabin cruiser *Cocktail II*	Saved boat + 3
11/5/1984	Fishing boats	Escorted boats
24/5/1984	Fishing boats	Escorted boats
10/8/1984	Motor fishing vessel	Saved boat + 2
19/9/1984	Fishing vessel *Aqua Star*	Saved boat + 2
15/11/1984	MFV's *Yellow Peril* & *My Girls*	Escorted boats
20/4/1985	*Force Four GT*	Saved boat + 2
13/5/1985	Fishing boats	Escorted boats
3/6/1965	Injured man on MV *Bandick* of Guernsey	Landed injured man
3/8/1985	Catamaran *Norwegian Blue*	Stood by
11/8/1985	Rafts	Saved 65
15/9/1985	Two scuba divers	Saved 2
23/6/1986D	Fishing vessel *Morning Rose*	Landed 3
7/7/1986D	Fishing vessel *Joan Elizabeth*	Gave help
9/7/1986D	Fishing vessel *Joan Elizabeth*	Gave help
8/8/1986D	Cabin cruiser *OB2*	Gave help
28/10/1986	*Crystal Dawn*	Saved boat + 2
25/4/1987	Fishing boat *Fragrance*	Gave help
28/5/1987	MFVs *Kathleen*, *Mizpah* & *Pegasus*	Gave help
28/5/1987	Fishing vessel *Good Courage*	Escorted boat
25/7/1987	MFVs *Pegasus* & *Donna Marie*	Escorted boats
29/7/1987	Fishing vessel *Sea Eagle*	Landed 3 sick men
4/10/1987	Fishing vessel *Cardine*	Saved 2
15/5/1988	Yacht *Kitaja*	Gave help
26/6/1988	Fishing vessel *Justifier*	Gave help
19/8/1988	Sailboard	Saved board + 1
21 9/1988	Fishing vessel *Liberty*	Gave help
15/2/1989	Ro-ro Cargo vessel *Tor Gothia* of Sweden	Stood by vessel
16/4/1989	Fishing boat *Cheryl C*	Saved boat + 2
30/5/1989	Fishing vessel *Pegasus* of Yarmouth	Escorted vessel
21/6/1989	MFVs *Donna Marie* & *Justifier*	Gave help
29/6/1989	Fishing vessel *Moonshine* of Grimsby	Gave help
30/7/1989	Yacht *Meg*	Saved boat + 3
30/7/1989	Sailing club safety boat *Jeanie*	Escorted boat
30/7/1989	Fishing vessel *Sea Eagle*	Escorted vessel
14/4/1990	Sailboard	Saved board +1
15/7/1990	Fishing boat *Blue Boy*	Gave help
19/8/1990	Skin diver	Saved 1
19/8/1990	2 Motor boats	Gave help
28/9/1990	Yacht *Smiling Swiss*	Landed injured woman

Sheringham Lifeboats
From 1990 to 2000

At the end of 1985, Sheringham's Oakley class lifeboat *The Manchester Unity of Oddfellows* was taken to Rochester in Kent for a refit. As there was no reserve offshore lifeboat available, a 'D' class inshore craft (number 204) was sent, which remained at Sheringham for just over six months and made four service launches, saving three lives.

When *Lloyds II*, Sheringham's last all-weather lifeboat, was withdrawn on 18th April 1992 a V class Atlantic 21 lifeboat was placed on station. B536 served from April 1992 to December 1993 and she was followed by B539 *Lions International*, which remained on duty for four months before being replaced by the new, permanent, Atlantic 75 class lifeboat *Manchester Unity of Oddfellows*. The B class lifeboats launched a total of eleven times on service.

Atlantic 75, *Manchester Unity of Oddfellows* carried out her first service launch on 1st April 1994 in deteriorating weather with the wind gusting to force 9. Three of the local crab boats were observed making their way westwards close inshore. Two of them were able to land but the third, the 17 foot *Alison Katherine*, was hit by a very heavy sea as it approached. The Atlantic 75 was launched in under eight minutes, a crew-member was transferred to the casualty to assist, and the *Alison Katherine* was towed to a position from which it could beach safely.

Another particularly arduous service took place on the 13th September 2000 in a moderate WNW wind in fine weather. The boat *Finarbed* with five persons and a dog on board, called for assistance when it began taking on water some 21 miles NNE of Sheringham. The lifeboat stood by until the boat was taken in tow to Yarmouth.

Over the last couple of years, the lifeboat has been called to assist a 75 foot beam trawler (the *Zuaderzee*), windsurfers, a light aircraft, walkers, and anglers among others. On the 24th October 2002, a call was received from Yarmouth Coastguard requesting that the *Manchester Unity of Oddfellows* be launched to the assistance of the *Quay Sweep*. This 18 foot crabber had capsized in the very heavy swell running at Blakeney harbour bar, throwing her crew of three into the water. The lifeboat located the casualties and their boat on the eastern side of Blakeney Point, and one of the lifeboatmen entered the water to assist two of the casualties into the lifeboat. He then assisted the third casualty to fix a line to the *Quay Sweep* and the lifeboat towed the crabber back to Morston Quay where the casualties were landed.

Alison Katherine
1st April, 1994

Clive Rayment: Coxswain A.L.B. 1989-1992
Senior Helmsman I.LB 1992-1997

On Friday 1st April, 1994 at 7.35am, Mrs Bennett Middleton telephoned the Hon. Sec. to inform him that local fishing boats were still at sea and conditions were deteriorating. The Hon. Sec. immediately notified Senior Helmsman Rayment and the two made their way to the Lifeboat house where they were able to see three single-handed, open skiffs beating westwards about 200 yards off Sheringham in heavy weather. All were approaching the area of the Fishermans Slope. The leading two boats were seen to run ashore safely, however, when the third boat commenced its run it was seen to take a very heavy sea and then flounder. The sole occupant was seen waving at the shore. The assembly signal was immediately sounded at 7.42am by the Hon. Sec., and the Senior Helmsman commenced readying the lifeboat. The crew assembled rapidly and the lifeboat was launched into rough seas at 7.50am. Meanwhile the casualty had managed to get its head to sea and was holding its position in heavy seas – obviously on reduced power. The lifeboat came alongside the skiff at 7.55am and DLA Holsey transferred to the casualty to assist Mr Neal to go ashore. It was found the casualty's engines had been swamped and was only running on one cylinder. A tow was passed from the lifeboat to the casualty, which was then towed towards the beach – a very dangerous manoeuvre as current sea defence works at Sheringham have required the placing of some 20,000 tons of large rocks along the beaches of Sheringham, leaving only a relatively narrow, unmarked channel through to the fisherman's beach when the tide is up and the rocks are underwater. Indeed the casualty was actually swept against the rocks as it passed them, suffering minor damage in the process.

When the casualty was close to the beach the tow was cast and the lifeboat made its way back out to sea heading directly into the gale. Conditions had become so bad that Senior Helsman Clive Rayment had to send his two crewmen forward to ballast the bow of the lifeboat against the lifting of the wind.

The lifeboat then stood by at sea whilst the coastguards checked beaches at West Runton and Weybourne to ensure that no more boats were at sea.

At 8.26am the lifeboat returned to station where conditions for recovery were far from ideal. A very strong sweep was running from West to East along the beach and the incoming tide was well advanced by the strong wind. Senior Helsman Rayment displayed great skill and seamanship in bringing the lifeboat safely ashore under very difficult circumstances with no room for error.

*Manchester Unity of Oddfellows on service to
the fishing boat Alison Katherine, 1994*

18ft Dory
18th May, 1999

On 18th May 1999 the *Manchester Unity of Oddfellows* was launched into an Easterly force 6. The lifeboat had been requested by Yarmouth Coastguard to go to Blakeney to locate a dory which had been lost to view trying to cross Blakeney bar. The lifeboat crew's first sighting was of the dory coming almost vertically off the top of a large wave. The two occupants seemed unaware of the danger they were in. They tried to convince the crew they could negotiate the bar. The crew convinced them to come ashore and took the dory in tow right up to the coastguard at Morston Creek.

*Manchester Unity of Oddfellows on service to 18ft Dory
off Blakeney, May 1999*

Services by the Sheringham Lifeboats 1990 to 2001

RNLB Lloyds II
1990-1992

Date	Vessel	Action
7/10/1990	Yacht *Lady of Thanet*	Gave help
4/6/1991	Fishing boat *Welcome Messenger*	Escorted boat
4/8/1991	Motor boat *Agar Spirit*	Gave help
7/9/1991	Body in sea	Landed a body
15/2/1992	Yacht *Tagimurlia*	Gave help
19/3/1992	Yacht *Chaos*	Gave help
23/3/1992	*Charles Mark* & *Northern Star*	Stood by boats

Atlantic 21
1992-1994

Date	Vessel	Action
18/6/1992	*Charles Mark* & *Northern Star*	Escorted boats
25/6/1992	Fishing vessel *Mary D*	Gave help
11/8/1992	Cabin cruiser *Ulster Queen*	Gave help
12/8/1992	Fishing boat	Escorted boat
5/9/1992	Flotation buoy	Gave help
29/1/1993	Fishing boat *My Girls II*	Escorted boat
21/3/1993	Yacht *Katina*	Gave help
11/4/1993	Fishing vessel *Tom-Kit*	Escorted vessel
23/5/1993	Sailing dinghy	Stood by boat
4/8/1993	Fishing vessel *Triton*	Gave help
23/9/1993	Fishing vessel *Verity Ellen*	Gave help

Atlantic 75
Manchester Unity of Oddfellows

Date	Vessel	Action
1/4/1994	Fishing boat *Alison Cathleen*	Saved boat + 1
20/5/1994	Fishing boat	Escorted boat
26/7/1994	Two sailboards	Gave help
27/11/1994	Barge *Polly*	Gave help
23/3/1995	Fishing vessel *Verity Ellen*	Craft + 1
12/4/1995	F.V. *Carrie Anne*	Craft + 2
21/4/1995	Fishing boat *Samara*	Craft + 1
25/4/1995	3 MFVs *Blue Boy*, *Scout* & *My Girls II*	Escorted boats
26/7/1995	F. Bts. *Blue Boy* & *My Girls II*	Escorted boats
28/5/1996	Fishing vessel *Laura Jane*	Saved boat +3
4/7/1196	Fishing vessel *Blue Boy*	Saved boat +1
11/9/1996	Fishing vessel *Blue Boy*	Saved boat +1
9/7/1997	Three divers	Saved 2
13/9/1997	Fishing vessels *Mizpah* and *Valery Theresa*	Escorted boats
25/2/1998	Injured man on fishing vessel *Katie Girl*	Landed injured
28/2/1998	Sailboard	Gave help
3/4/1998	Fishing vessels *Anna Gail*, *Sarah Jane*, *Verity Ellen* & *Sheila Joyce*	Escorted boats
22/5/1998	Fishing vessels	Stood by
29/5/1998	Fishing vessels	Escorted boats
24/8/1998	Motor Cruiser *Fairlie Knackered*	Escorted craft
29/9/1998	Yacht *Sissi*	Saved craft + 1
14/10/1998	Fishing vessel *Johnathan James*	Saved boat +2
5/4/1999	Yacht	Saved craft + 1
6/5/1999	Fishing vessels	Escorted boats
18/5/1999	Motor boat	Saved boat + 2
10/7/1999	Six divers	Saved 6
10/7/1999	Diver support craft *Desert Moon*	Stood by craft
2/8/1999	Two divers	Saved 2
6/9/1999	Two people stranded	Saved 2
14/3/2000	Fishing vessel *Tradewinds*	Stood by
13/4/2000	Fishing vessels	Escorted boats
24/4/2000	Power boat	Saved boat + 2
27/5/2000	Motorboat *Minuet*	Stood by
28/5/2000	Yacht *Panther*	Escorted craft
6/8/2000	Speedboat *Diminished Responsibility*	Saved boat + 3
27/8/2000	Powerboat *Independence*	Saved boat + 7
12/9/2000	Fishing vessel *Lynn Anne*	Gave help
13/9/2000	Fishing vessel *Fin-ar-bed*	Assisted to save vessel
23/3/2001	Fishing vessel *Tradewinds*	Escorted boat
4/4/2001	Fishing vessel *Providence II*	Escorted boat
7/8/2001	Jet ski	Saved craft + 1
7/8/2001	Canoe	Saved craft +1
24/8/2001	Powerboat	Saved craft +3
26/8/2001	Sick divers on dive support craft *Calypso*	1 life saved 2 landed
26/8/2001	Dive support craft *Calypso*	Saved craft + 2
12/9/2001	Jet ski	Saved craft + 1

Acknowledgements

I wish to thank the following for their help in the creation of this book:

Henry 'Joyful' West for a fine foreword and his knowledge of the North Sea

Robin and Linda West for a great introduction and the use of their research and text

Chris Howden for his thorough proof reading

Chromatics of Hove for the trannies

Brian Farrow for access to the RNLI records

Nina for the typesetting

Micky Gunn and the gang at Hartington Fine Arts for the print.

Thanks also to Brian Pegg, Jack West, Peter Brooks, Martyn Jackson, Clive Rayment, Richard Little and Steven Neal

Bibliography

West R&L. *The Story of the Sheringham Lifeboats*, Robin and Linda West, 1996

Cox P. & Groves T. *The Fishermen's Lifeboat*, Sheringham Town Council, 1994

Johnson H.R. *One Hundred Years of Lifeboat Service at Sheringham*, RNLI, 1936

RNLI, *Service Reports of the Sheringham Lifeboats*

RNLI Awards
to the Sheringham Lifeboatmen

R.N.L.I Silver Medal
Coxswain H. "Downtide" West	31.10.1956	*S.S. Wimbledon*

R.N.L.I Bronze Medals
Coxswain J. Dumble	29.10.1941	*S.S. Eaglescliffe Hall*
Motor Mechanic E.C. Craske	31.10.1956	*S.S. Wimbledon*
Helmsman C. Rayment (Cromer ILB)	01.05.1981	*George William*

Thanks of the R.N.L.I on Vellum
Coxswain H. "Downtide" West	19.05.1955	*S.S. Zor*
Crew members:	H. Bishop	31.10.1956	*S.S. Wimbledon*
	A. Scotter	31.10.1956	*S.S. Wimbledon*
	J.H. Bishop	31.10.1956	*S.S. Wimbledon*
	D. Little	31.10.1956	*S.S. Wimbledon*
	R. Little	31.10.1956	*S.S. Wimbledon*
	R. West	31.10.1956	*S.S. Wimbledon*
Coxswain	H. "Downtide" West	15.08.1961	*Lucy*
2nd Coxswain	H. "Joyful" West	15.08.1961	*Lucy*
Bowman	A. Scotter	15.08.1961	*Lucy*
Crewman	E. Wink	15.08.1961	*Lucy*

Letters of Congratulations
Acting Coxswain J. West	04.09.1976	Barge *Focena*
7 Local Fishermen	29.08.1981	2 men rescued from sea
Coxswain J. West	15.09.1985	2 divers rescued
Mr. D. Williams	Oct. 1987	Rescue of a drowning man

Silver Statuette for Long Service
Mr. H. "Downtide" West	1973
Mr. H. "Joyful" West	1996

Special Honours
Coxswain H. "Joyful" West	B.E.M.	June 1982
Coxswain Mechanic B. Pegg	B.E.M.	June 1989

James Bower Endowment Award
Coxswain H. "Downtide" West: First co-recipient of an award from this fund after winning the RNLI's Silver Medal in 1956.